by Joseph J. Arpad
& Kenneth R. Lincoln

FILTER PRESS
Palmer Lake, Colorado 80133
1971

FILTER PRESS
Wild And Woolly West BOOKS

Phone 719-481-2523

P.O. Box 5, Palmer Lake, Colorado 80133

1.	Choda	Thirty Pound Rails, 1956
2.	Clemens	Celebrated Jumping Frog, 1965
3.	Banks	Uncle Jim's Book of Pancakes, 1967, 1979
4.	Service	Yukon Poems, 1967
5.	Cushing	My Adventures in Zuni, 1967
6.	Englert	Oliver Perry Wiggins, 1968 *(Out of Print)*
7.	Matthews	Navajo Weavers & Silversmiths, 1968
8.	Campbell	West Plates & Dry Gulches, 1970
9.	Banks	Alferd Packer's Wilderness Cookbook, 1969
10.	Faulk	Simple Methods of Mining Gold, 1969, 1981
11.	Rusho	Powell's Canyon Voyage, 1969
12.	Hinckley	Transcontinental Rails, 1969
13.	Young	The Grand Canyon, 1969
14.	Gehm	Nevada's Yesterdays, 1970 *(Out of Print)*
15.	Seig	Tobacco, Peace Pipes, & Indians, 1971
16.	Conrotto	Game Cookery Recipes, 1971 *(Out of Print)*
17.	Scanland	Life of Pat F. Garrett, 1971
18.	Hunt	High Country Ghost Town Poems, 1962, 1971 *(Out of Print)*
19.	Arpad	Buffalo Bill's Wild West, 1971
20.	Wheeler	Deadwood Dick's Leadville Lay, 1971 *(Out of Print)*
21.	Powell	The Hopi Villages, 1972
22.	Bathke	The West in Postage Stamps, 1973 *(Out of Print)*
23.	Hesse	Southwestern Indian Recipe Book, 1973
24.	Vangen	Indian Weapons, 1972 *(Out of Print)*
25.	MacDonald	Cockeyed Charley Parkhurst, 1973 *(Out of Print)*
26.	Schwatka	Among the Apaches, 1974
27.	Bourke	General Crook in the Indian Country *and*
	Remington	A Scout with the Buffalo Soldiers, 1974
28.	Powell	An Overland Trip to the Grand Canyon, 1974
29.	Harte	Luck of Roaring Camp & other sketches, 1975
30.	Remington	On the Apache Reservations & Among the Cheyennes, 1974
31.	Ferrin	Many Moons Ago, 1976 *(Out of Print)*
32.	Kirby	Saga of Butch Cassidy, 1977 *(Out of Print)*
33.	Isom	Fox Grapes, Cherokee Verse, 1977 *(Out of Print)*
34.	Bryan	Navajo Native Dyes, 1978
35.	deBaca	Vicente Silva, Terror of Las Vegas, 1978
36.	Underhill	Pueblo Crafts, 1979
37.	Underhill	Papago & Pima Indians of Arizona, 1979
38.	Riker	Colorado Ghost Towns & Mining Camps, 1979 *(Out of Print)*
39.	Bennett	Genuine Navajo Rug; How to Tell, 1979
40.	Duran	Blonde Chicana Bride's Mexican Cookbook, 1981
41.	Kennard	Field Mouse Goes to War, 1977
42.	Keasey	Gadsden's Silent Observers, 1974
43.	Beshoar	Violet Soup, 1982 *(Out of Print)*
44.	Underhill	People of the Crimson Evening, 1982
45.	Choda	West on Wood, 5 vols. *(In preparation)*
46.	Duran	Mexican Recipe Shortcuts, 1983
47.	Roosevelt	Frontier Types in Cowboy Land, 1988

ISBN 0-910584-62-1 paper
L.C #73-106990

PRINTED IN THE UNITED STATES OF AMERICA

912
001 002 003 004 005 006 007 008 009 010 011 012

½

INTRODUCTION

In our popular lore, the cowboy is "the good guy," the Indian, his natural opponent. But during most of the nineteenth century, they were both feared by Americans – at best, as "bad men to fool with," at worst, as killers. As late as 1881, President Chester A. Arthur, in a message to Congress, not only affirmed a continued policy of Indian suppression but also asked for legislation to subdue "these armed desperadoes" known as "Cow-boys" who were tyrannizing the West. Within a decade, however, the emergence of *Buffalo Bill's Wild West* reversed this national attitude by transforming the cowboy from a no-account ruffian into a cultural hero, while at the same time promoting the Indian as "An Enemy in '76, A Friend in '85." Perhaps, more than any other single event, Buffalo Bill's western extravaganza packaged and made respectable "the wild and woolly West."

ROUTE-BOOK

Buffalo Bill's Wild West

1899.

Colon. W. F. Cody-"Buffalo Bill".

Miss Annie Oakley. — Black Heart, Indian chief.

EDITORIAL NOTE

The editors wish to thank the Library of Congress; the Bancroft Library, University of California at Berkeley; the Special Collections Division, University of California at Los Angeles Library; and the Huntington Library for making materials available for use in this book. A fully detailed account of Cody's Wild West show may be found in Henry Blackman Sell and Victor Weybright, *Buffalo Bill and the Wild West* (New York: Oxford University Press, 1955). Cody's autobiography, *The Life of the Honorable William F. Cody* (Hartford, Conn.: F. E. Bliss, 1879), is exaggerated but, nevertheless, the starting point for any investigation of the showman's character. Richard J. Walsh's *The Making of Buffalo Bill: A Study in Heroics* (New York: D. Appleton and Co., 1920), written in collaboration with Milton S. ("Nate") Salsbury, draws a portrait of the man behind the legend, using material supplied by Cody's partner. Henry Nash Smith, in *Virgin Land: The American West as Symbol and Myth* (Cambridge, Mass.: Harvard University Press, 1950), analyzes the Buffalo Bill legend created in popular literature. Benjamin A. Botkin, in *A Treasury of American Folklore* (New York: Crown Publishers, 1944), looks at the Wild West show and its proprietor in the context of American folk traditions. John G. Neihardt's *Black Elk Speaks* (Lincoln, Neb.; University of Nebraska Press, 1961) gives a look at the Wild West show from an Indian participant's point of view. Finally, the Buffalo Bill Museum and the Whitney Gallery of Western Art, both in Cody, Wyoming, contain innumerable artifacts of Buffalo Bill's Wild West.

HON. W. F. CODY, (BUFFALO BILL.)

CHARGING BACK TO THE RESCUE.

A MAGNIFICENT CHARGE.

NATE SALSBURY.

TEXAS JACK (J. B. OMOHUNDRO).

When William Frederick Cody launched his *Wild West* show, he had already won fame as the legendary scout, horseman, and sharp-shooter, "Buffalo Bill." Born in Le Claire, Iowa, on February 26, 1846, he had gone westering with his family along the gold rush highway to Salt Creek valley in Kansas. There, Will's father, who opposed slavery, was knifed in the back for voicing his sentiments in public; he died in 1857 during the John Brown frenzy. At the age of eleven, young Will suddenly became the family breadwinner. Finding work as a scout for a wagon train, he allegedly killed a hostile Indian and gained a reputation as "the youngest Indian slayer of the plains." At the age of fourteen, he rode with the Pony Express and, during its short seventeen-month existence, began to traffic with such characters as Jim Bridger, Kit Carson, and Wild Bill Hickok. He gained notoriety as a buffalo hunter in his early twenties when astride "Brigham," his first buffalo-hunting horse, and carrying "Lucretia Borgia," his breech-loading Springfield rifle, he hired on with the Kansas Pacific Railway to scout for Indians and to supply the rail crews with meat. In 1869, he reportedly won a $500 bet by killing 69 buffalo in eight hours. Within 17 months, he had slaughtered 4,280 buffalo in all.

As it happened, Ned Buntline (E. Z. C. Judson), one of the most prolific and successful of the dime novelists at the time, was in the West looking for a new hero to glorify in his pulp fictions. He stumbled across Cody at Fort McPherson, Kansas, and quickly celebrated the buffalo hunter in a serial for the *New York Weekly,* dubbing him "Buffalo Bill, the King of the Bordermen." Republished as a novel, the saga of Buffalo Bill so fascinated Eastern readers that, in 1872, Fred G. Maeder capitalized on the vogue by dramatizing the budding legend for the New York Bowery Theater. In the same year, James Gordon Bennett, the publicity-seeking editor of the *New York Herald,* invited Cody to attend the play in New York – which he did, to the enthusiastic applause of the audience. By the end of the same year, Cody was coaxed into playing himself in the Chicago production of Buntline's play, *Scouts of the Plains.* The performance enraged drama critics but enthralled the audience, as the "actors" (Cody, Buntline, "Texas Jack" Omohundro, and a dozen or so mock Indians) extemporized forgotten lines into an impromptu Western melodrama. Stage struck by his popularity as "Bison William," Cody continued in the role, fattening the plot with old cronies like Wild Bill Hickok and thrilling the audiences with ad lib, rough-and-tumble spectacles.

But while a glamorous image on the Eastern stage, Cody yearned to make a full-dress appearance in the "wild West" where he began. Thus, when the news of Sitting Bull's 1876 uprising reached him in

BRINGING LIVE MEAT INTO CAMP.

BEHIND THE FOOTLIGHTS.

SITTING BULL.

THE FINDING OF CUSTER'S BODY.

Wilmington, he rushed onto the stage shouting to the audience that he was through acting Indian warfare – that he was returning to the frontier to fight in a real Indian war. He boarded the first train out of town and four days later arrived in the West to enlist as a cavalry scout. Too late for the Battle of Little Big Horn on June 25, he still claimed first vengeance for Custer three weeks later when he slew Yellow Hand, a Cheyenne warrior, and "scientifically scalped him in about five seconds" (as he wrote in his autobiography) – still wearing his Wilmington stage dress, a Mexican suit of black velvet, slashed with scarlet and trimmed with silver buttons and lace. Six weeks later, he was back in Rochester, wearing the same costume while re-enacting the drama of the Yellow Hand duel in the free and easy format of Buntline's play. Thereafter, he so promoted himself as part of the Custer legend that the Plains Indians came to regard him as "the other Pahuska" (meaning "Long-hair"), the original being Custer himself.

Death of Yellow Hand—"The first scalp for Custer."

THE LAST ONE OF CUSTER'S BRAVE BAND.

GIVING ROYALTY A SPIN DURING AN ATTACK BY INDIANS.

II

Cody's flare for mixing theatrics and real life led him quite naturally to the creation of *Buffalo Bill's Wild West.* In 1882, when he began the show, the "wild West" was rapidly passing into memory – the buffalo were gone, the Indian uprisings were over, and men like Kit Carson and Wild Bill Hickok were dead. Cody himself had slipped into semi-retirement, settling into a residence he called "Welcome Wigwam" near North Platte, Nebraska. But as the Fourth of July approached, the townspeople invited Cody to officiate at an "Old Glory Blowout," a competition of round-up events (bronc riding, steer roping, sharp shooting, and other cowboy stunts) that had become popular in the West as early as 1869 as a way of celebrating Independence Day. Cody rose to the occasion with his own sense of theatrics. To the traditional events he added horse races, a drive of a small herd of buffalo, and an Indian attack on the Deadwood stage coach. The resulting "Blow Out" proved so successful (he had circulated handbills expecting about a hundred cowboys to respond, but over a thousand appeared on the day of the event) that he and his friend, Nate Salsbury, a New York actor, decided to take the show east. Within three years, they were grossing over a million dollars annually with their show. After four years, Cody owned his own train of white railroad cars with his name emblazoned in gold letters on the sides. As his publicity agent boasted, Cody "out-Barnumed Barnum."

The show, however, was not quite a circus, and it was more than a rodeo. In fact, the term "show" was never used to describe it. Instead, Cody simply called it his "Wild West," as though somehow, miraculously, he had transported the living West to the east for public examination. The script of the spectacle, which this book reproduces, gives some idea of the show's performance; Cody and Salsbury deposited the script in the Library of Congress in 1883 when they copyrighted their newly created "Blow Out." The illustrations used herein are also drawn from the original programs for the show. Those by Charles Henckel are especially noteworthy for they were drawn by a German artist who had never seen the American West. Henckel imagined the scenes after seeing the *Wild West* during its European tour, and Cody so admired them that he had them done up into a little book which he sold as a souvenir of his *Wild West* performances.

Cody continually changed the script of his *Wild West* in an attempt to outdo himself, but he always retained two basic elements: the exhibitions of Indian and cowboy skills (foot racing, riding, lassoing, and shooting); and the dramatic portraits of life in the West (the Pony Express, the Indian dances and ceremonies, Custer's Last Stand, and the burning of a settler's cabin by Indians). Despite the music and stage trappings, these events acquired a heightened realism because, as the handbills proclaimed, the *Wild West* always featured "Everything Genuine!" – the original Deadwood stage coach and the actual Indian warriors (Sitting Bull, Spotted Tail, and Rain-in-the-Face) who had fought in the West. Mingled with the authentic, however, were characters out of the dime novels of the period – "Broncho Bill" and "Con Croner, the Cowboy Sheriff of the Platte," not to mention "Buffalo Bill" himself. The effect was a captivating illusion of reality, one that denied skeptical detachment. The spectator had the sense that he was actually witnessing an historical moment or seeing a legend come to life.

The Deadwood stage coach proved a particularly useful vehicle for transporting people into the romance of the West. With superb showmanship, Cody would invite distinguished members of the audience to ride in the coach to its destined attack by Indians. When the show played an 1887 command performance at Windsor Castle in England to celebrate Queen Victoria's Golden Jubilee, the Prince of Wales rode shotgun as Buffalo Bill drove his passengers (the Kings of Greece, Saxony, Denmark, and Belgium) to safety while the U.S. Cavalry repelled a bloodcurdling attack by Wild West renegades. And at the 1889 World's Fair in Paris, the Deadwood stage saved the Shah of Persia and ex-Queen of Spain, Isabella, from the marauding savages. When Pope Leo XIII invited the Wild West Company to the Vatican, Cody toyed with the idea of racing the Deadwood stage coach in the Roman Coliseum until he arrived and found it cluttered with stone; he settled, instead, for a photograph of the Buffalo Bill troupe in the ancient arena. Likewise, when the 1889 tour ended in Venice, the Deadwood stage gave way to gondolas, as the Wild West entourage paraded through the city canals.

Graced by the patronage of Old World aristocracy, the "cowboy fun" of the *Wild West* no longer seemed disreputable. At the 1893 World's Fair in Chicago, the President of the United States, Grover Cleveland, opened the show, and Cody introduced a feature that another President would imitate five years later in the Spanish American War, "The Congress of Rough Riders of the World" – a dress parade of equestrian troops from America, England, France, Germany and Russia. As the Buffalo Bill cult reached its zenith, Cody became Teddy Roosevelt's personal hero, while posters for the show compared Buffalo Bill, "The Man on Horse 1895," with Napoleon, "The Man on Horse 1795." Meanwhile, within the show as it played in America, the horse races no longer pitted cowboys against Indians, but instead contested a cowboy against a Russian Cossack, a Mexican vaquero, and an Arabian horseman – with the fate and honor of the nation riding in

Indians on the prairie.

Les indiens sur les plaines de l'Ouest. — Indianische Häuptlinge in der Prairie.

SCOUTING AMONG THE CIVILIANS.

Emigrant-train attacked by Indians.

Cortège d'emigrés attaqué par des Indiens. — Emigrantenzug von Indianern überfallen.

the balance, to be confirmed by the new American hero from the West.

Thus, Cody, as Buffalo Bill, almost single-handedly reversed the public's attitude toward the cowboy. Although he had killed several Indians, he had never shot a white man, so the term "killer" was never applied to him. In the literary hands of Buntline and Colonel Prentiss Ingraham (who wrote more than 200 stories about Buffalo Bill), Cody became a genteel reincarnation of James Fenimore Cooper's frontier hero, Leatherstocking – dressed, however, in exotic attire reflective of Victorian tastes. In one dime novel, for example, he wore "a red velvet jacket, white corduroy pants, stuck into handsome top boots armed with heavy gold spurs, and a gray sombrero, encircled by a gold cord and looped up on the left side with a pin representing a spur." In another, he wore "an embroidered silk shirt, a black cravat, gauntlet gloves, and a sash of red silk, in which were stuck a pair of revolvers and a dirk-knife." This dress, of course, was foreign to Cody. But he found that Eastern audiences expected him to wear such regalia when he took to the stage. Much to his own pleasure, he discovered that he enjoyed the plumage and thereafter made exotic costuming a featured part of his dramatic performances. Far from mocking him as a "dandy," the home-spun natives back West feted him with the title "Honorable" by electing him to the Nebraska State Legislature in 1872; the Governor appointed him "Colonel" in the National Guard some time later. Though Cody never served in these capacities, he made good use of the titles to legitimatize and elevate his *Wild West* entertainment: he was always introduced as "the Honorable William F. Cody" or "Colonel Cody," and he marshalled the performance as though he were a distinguished statesman or a military general. This is not to say that he lorded over the company. Annie Oakley was treated like a lady, despite the unlady-like nature of her profession; the performers were all "champions," "first-rate," or "first-class," and treated with due respect. The effect was one of a big happy family, an idyllic picture of genteel domesticity – Sitting Bull, in fact, adopted Annie Oakley as his daughter, naming her "Little Sure Shot."

But although the Indians were part of the Wild West family, they were regarded with what can best be described as ambivalence. Sitting Bull, for example, was heralded as a military genius, the equal of any white general. But balanced against the moment of his glory in the re-enacted Battle of Little Big Horn was the dramatization of the Death of Yellow Hand in revenge for Custer's defeat. Likewise, balanced against the exhibitions of skill and the ceremonials that pictured the Indians as men of talent and virtue were the scenes of savagery – the attacks on emigrant trains, the Deadwood stage coach, and the settler's cabin. Cody's own attitude toward the Indians may have been reflected

OUR DEPARTURE FOR ENGLAND.

in this ambivalence. For instance, during his European tour, he proudly exhibited Black Elk, a holy man for the Oglala Sioux, as an exotic example of the Indian character. But when Queen Victoria, speaking to Black Elk and his followers at her Golden Jubilee command performance, told them "today I have seen the best-looking people I know" and that "if you belonged to me, I would not let them take you around in a show like this," Cody must have felt offended. Shortly thereafter, when the show left for the continent to continue its tour, Cody abandoned Black Elk and several other Indians in the streets of Manchester. Lost and knowing none of the white man's languages, Black Elk wandered for two years through England, France, and Germany before finding his way back to the touring Buffalo Bill troupe – whereupon Cody welcomed him like a long lost brother and had the troupe send up three cheers for his safe reunion.

Buffalo Bill 's
defunct
                who used to
                ride a watersmooth-silver
                                                  stallion
and break onetwothreefourfive pigeonsjustlikethat
                                                                      Jesus

he was a handsome man
                                  and what i want to know is
how do you like your blueeyed boy
Mister Death

SALUTING HER MAJESTY, QUEEN VICTORIA.

III

Cody managed and starred in his *Wild West* for thirty years, from 1883 to 1913. Although he always tried to distinguish his show from a circus, the difference grew negligible in later years. Starting in 1898, he added sideshow attractions – a snake charmer, a sword swallower, a boy giant, a Kaffir warrior, jugglers, midgets, Venetian glass blowers – upon the advice of his new partner, James A. Bailey, of later Barnum and Bailey fame. By 1909, the cover of the program illustrated Buffalo Bill with Pawnee Bill, another new partner, surrounded by elephants and Indians. These later dimensions, bizarre and perhaps cheapening, foreshadowed the day in 1913 when Cody, in financial stress, was forced to merge with the Sells-Floto Circus.

The decline of the *Wild West* was partly a mark of its success. Once the cowboy was respectable and the Indian made as attractive as repulsive, a large part of the thrill of seeing them in action was lost. In addition, new art forms emerged that could carry the excitement of the West to the people with greater efficiency and less cost. In 1902, for instance, Owen Wister published *The Virginian*, frequently recognized as the first "Western," a genre of literature that ritualized many of the scenes included in Cody's *Wild West*, but with much greater scope and immediacy than could be achieved in the arena. A year later, Edwin S. Porter produced *The Great Train Robbery*, considered the first successful motion picture, which allowed everyone to experience the thrill of being "held up," not just the Deadwood stage coach celebrities. Although Cody experimented with cycloramas and other scenic stage devices, he could not match the view of the West available through film. In 1913, he tried to adapt to the new medium to recoup his losses, contracting with Essanay of Hollywood to film *Mercaldo*, a history of the Indian wars at Wounded Knee in South Dakota. But his Sioux friends were none too happy about the venture, since the graves of their families massacred at Wounded Knee were only 23 years old; indeed, the Sioux talked of using live ammunition in the filming of the battle scenes. Though he completed the film, Cody failed to cover his debts, and he returned to the circus to play, until his death on January 10, 1917, the more predictable though somewhat diminished role of Buffalo Bill.

In the cultural changes from Cody's day to the present, dark comedy undermines pageantry, the theater of alienation upstages melodrama, and the problematic replaces the heroic. As late as 1946, Buffalo Bill could still sing "There's No Business Like Show Business" in the musical *Annie Get Your Gun*; but he rides a stick horse in Arthur Kopit's recent surrealistic drama, *Indians*, and hallucinates the slaughter of buffalo and Indians. Perhaps, Buffalo Bill is "defunct," as E. E.

Cummings claims, but while he lived, he had the power, as Carl Sandburg tells us, to make the boy heart of America ache with the romance of the West.

BUFFALO BILL

Boy heart of Johnny Jones—aching to-day?
Aching, and Buffalo Bill in town?
Buffalo Bill and ponies, cowboys, Indians?

Some of us know
All about it, Johnny Jones.

Buffalo Bill is a slanting look of the eyes,
  A slanting look under a hat on a horse.
He sits on a horse and a passing look is fixed
  On Johnny Jones, you and me, barelegged,
A slanting, passing, careless look under a hat on a horse.

Go clickety-clack, O pony hoofs along the street.
Come on and slant your eyes again, O Buffalo Bill.
Give us again the ache of our boy hearts.
Fill us again with the red love of prairies, dark nights,
    lonely wagons, and the crack-crack of rifles sputter-
    ing flashes into an ambush.

BUFFALO BILL'S "WILD WEST"
PRAIRIE EXHIBITION, AND ROCKY MOUNTAIN SHOW
A DRAMATIC-EQUESTRIAN EXPOSITION
OF
LIFE ON THE PLAINS,
WITH ACCOMPANYING MONOLOGUE AND
INCIDENTAL MUSIC
THE WHOLE INVENTED AND ARRANGED BY
W. F. CODY

W. F. CODY AND N. SALSBURY, PROPRIETORS AND MANAGERS
WHO HEREBY CLAIM AS THEIR SPECIAL PROPERTY
THE VARIOUS EFFECTS INTRODUCED IN
THE PUBLIC PERFORMANCES
OF
BUFFALO BILL'S "WILD WEST"
(1883)

Attack on a settler's cabin.

Attaque d'une cabane de colonistc. — Überfall eines Blockhauses.

MONOLOGUE

LADIES AND GENTLEMEN:

I desire to call your attention to an important fact. From time to time it will be my pleasure to announce to you the different features of the programme as they occur. In order that I may do so intelligently, I respectfully request your silence and attention while I am speaking. Our agents will pass among you with the biographical history of the life of Hon. William F. Cody ("Buffalo Bill") and other celebrities who will appear before you this afternoon. The Management desires to vouch for the truth and accuracy of all the statements contained in this book, and respectfully submitted to your attention, as helping you to understand and appreciate our entertainment. Before the entertainment begins, however, I wish to impress upon your minds that what you are about to witness is not a performance in the common sense of that term, but an exhibition of skill on the part of men who have acquired that quality while gaining a livelihood. Many unthinking people suppose that the different features of our exhibition are the result of what is technically called "rehearsals." Such, however, is not the fact, and anyone who witnesses our performance the second time will observe that men and animals alike are the creatures of circumstances, depending for their success upon their own skill, daring, and sagacity. In the East, the few who excel are known to all. In the far West, the names we offer to you this afternoon are the synonyms of skill, courage, and individual excellence. At the conclusion of the next overture our performance will commence with a grand processional parade of the "Wild West."

Overture, grand processional parade of cowboys, Mexicans, and Indians, with incidental music.

I will introduce the different groups and individual celebrities as they pass before you in review.

Enter a group of Pawnee Indians. Music. Enter Chief. Music. Enter a group of Mexican vaqueros. Music. Enter a group of Wichita Indians. Music. Enter Chief. Music. Enter a group of American Cowboys. Music. Enter King of Cowboys. Music. Enter Cowboy Sheriff of the Platte. Music. Enter a group of Sioux Indians. Music. Enter Chief. Music.

I next have the honor of introducing to your attention a man whose record as servant of the government, whose skill and daring as a frontiersman, whose place in history as the chief of scouts of the United States Army under such generals as Sherman, Sheridan, Hancock, Terry, Miles, Hazen, Royal, Merrit, Crook, Carr and others, and whose name as one of the avengers of the lamented Custer, and whose adherence throughout an eventful life to his chosen principle of

Buffalo-hunt.

Chasse aux buffles. — Büffeljagd.

"true to friend and foe," have made him well and popularly known throughout the world. You all know to whom I allude – the Honorable William F. Cody, "Buffalo Bill."

Enter Cody. Bugle Call. Cody speaks.

Ladies and Gentlemen: Allow me to introduce the equestrian portion of the Wild West Exhibition.

Turns to review.

Wild West, are you ready? Go!

Exeunt omnes.

First on our programme, a ________ mile race, between a cowboy, a Mexican, and an Indian, starting at ________ . You will please notice that these horses carry the heaviest trapping, and that neither of the riders weighs less than 145 pounds.

Next on our programme, the Pony Express. The Pony Express was established long before the Union Pacific Railroad was built across the continent, or even before the telegraph poles were set, and when Abraham Lincoln was elected President of the United States, it was important that the election returns from California should be brought across the mountains as quickly as possible. Mr. William Russell, the great government freighter, who at the time was in Washington, first proposed the Pony Express. He was told that it would take too long – 17 or 18 days. The result was a wager of $200,000 that the time could be made in less than ten days, and it was, the actual time being nine days, seventeen hours, leaving seven hours to spare, and winning the wager of two hundred thousand dollars. Mr. Billy Johnson will illustrate the mode of riding the Pony Express, mounting, dismounting, and changing the mail to fresh horses.

Music. Enter express rider, changing horses in front of the grandstand, and exit.

Next on our programme, a one hundred yard race between an Indian on foot and an Indian on an Indian pony, starting at a given point, running fifty yards, and returning to the starting point – virtually a race of a hundred yards.

Race as described above. Music.

GOVERNMENT MULE TEAM.

Next on our programme, an historical representation between Buffalo Bill and Yellow Hand, fought during the Sitting Bull war, on the 17th of July, 1876, at War Bonnet Creek, Dakota, shortly after the massacre of Custer. This fight was witnessed by General Carr's command and the Sioux army, and resulted in the death of Yellow Hand, and the first scalp taken in revenge of Custer's fate.

Duel as described above. Cody, supported by cowboys, etc., Yellow Hand by Indians. Music.

I have the pleasure of introducing Mr. Seth Clover. Mr. Clover will give an exhibition of his skill, shooting with a Winchester repeating rifle, at composition balls thrown from the hand.

Clover shoots as above.

Shooting two balls thrown in the air at the same time. You will notice that Mr. Clover is obliged to replace the discharged cartridge before he can shoot at the second ball.

Shoots as above.

Obscuring the sight by placing a card over the rifle.

Shoots as above.

If any gentleman has a half-dollar he would like to have mutilated and take home as a pocket piece, if he will throw it in upon the track, where we can get it, Mr. Clover will try and oblige him.

Shoots coin as above.

Shooting at a nickel.

Shoots as above.

Shooting at a marble. You will notice that the mark is hardly larger than the bullet shot at it.

Shoots as above.

Shooting a number of composition balls thrown in rapid succession.

Shoots as above. Exit.

I have the pleasure of introducing Master Johnny Baker, of North Platte, Neb., known as the Cowboy Kid. Master Johnny is 16 years of age, and the holder of the boy's champion badge for rifle and revolver shooting, and stands ready to meet any opponent of his age. Master Baker will give an exhibition of his skill, holding his rifle in various positions.

Holding the rifle sideways.

Holding the rifle to the left shoulder.

Cowboys riding bucking horses.

Cowboys montant les chevaux réticents. — Reiten von Bockpferden.

Holding the rifle upside down, on the top of his head.
Standing with his back to the target, bending forward, and shooting between his knees.
Leaning backward, over a support, and shooting over his head.
Standing with his back to the target, and taking aim by the aid of a small mirror.
Shooting composition balls thrown in air.

Shoots each shot as above. Exit.

Miss Annie Oakley, the celebrated wing and rifle shot. Miss Oakley will give an exhibition of her skill, shooting with a shot gun at Ligowsky patent clay pigeons, holding the gun in various positions.

Shoots pigeons sprung from trap.

Shooting double, from two traps sprung at the same time.

Shoots as above.

Picking the gun from the ground after the trap is sprung.

Shoots as above.

Shooting double in the same manner.

Shoots as above.

Shooting three composition balls, thrown in the air in rapid succession, the first with the rifle held upside down upon the head, the second and the third with the shot gun.

Shoots as above. Exit.

Next on our programme, the cowboy's fun, or the riding of bucking ponies and mules, by Mr. ________ , Mr. ________ , and Mr. ________ . There is an impression in the minds of many people that these horses are taught or trained to buck, or that they are compelled to do so by having foreign substances placed under their saddles. This, however, is not the fact. Bucking, the same as balking or running away, is a natural trait of the animal, confirmed by habit.

Riders announced, and mount in succession.

Watch Mr. Taylor pick up his hat.

Taylor rides past at full speed, leans out of his saddle and picks hat from the ground.

Watch Mr. Taylor pick up his handkerchief.

Taylor rides past at full speed, leans out of his saddle, and picks up handkerchief.

OVERLAND STAGE COACH.

Hon. William F. Cody, champion all round shot of the world.

Enter Mr. Cody.

Mr. Cody will give an exhibition of his skill, shooting with shot gun, rifle and revolver at clay pigeons and composition balls, shooting first with a shot gun at clay pigeons, pulling the traps himself. (*Shoots.*) Shooting clay pigeons in the American style of holding the gun, the butt of the gun below his elbow. (*Shoots.*) Shooting clay pigeons in the English style of holding the gun, the butt of the gun below the armpit. Please notice the change of position. (*Shoots.*)

Shooting clay pigeons standing with his back to the trap, turning and breaking the pigeon while it is in the air. (*Shoots.*)

Shooting with his back to the trap, gun over his shoulder, turning and pulling the traps himself. (*Shoots.*)

Holding the gun with one hand. (*Shoots.*)

Holding the gun with one hand, pulling the trap with the other. (*Shoots.*)

Shooting clay pigeons double from two traps sprung at the same time. (*Shoots.*)

Shooting clay pigeons double, pulling the traps himself. (*Shoots.*)

Shooting twenty clay pigeons inside of one minute and thirty seconds. Any gentleman desiring to hold the time on this feat will please take it, not from the pulling of the trap, but from the first crack of the gun. (*Shoots.*)

Mr. Cody will shoot next with a Winchester repeating rifle, at composition balls, thrown from the hand while he rides upon his horse. (*Shoots.*) Missing with the first shot, hitting with the second. (*Shoots.*)

Missing twice, hitting the third time. (*Shoots.*)

Hitting three balls thrown in the air at the same time. (*Shoots.*)

Hitting a ball thrown from behind. (*Shoots.*)

Hitting a ball thrown to either side. (*Shoots.*)

Hitting a number of balls thrown in the air in rapid succession. (*Shoots.*)

Hitting a ball thrown in the air while he rides past it at full speed, a shot accomplished by no other marksman. (*Shoots.*)

Mr. Cody will next attempt the great double shot, hitting two balls thrown in the air at the same time. (*Shoots.*)

Mr. Cody will next attempt the great double shot! Hitting two balls thrown in the air at the same time, as he rides past at full speed. (*Shoots.*)

Hitting composition balls thrown in the air, while marksman and object thrower ride side by side at full speed, thus forming a picture of combined horsemanship and marksmanship never before presented to a public audience. (*Shoots.*)

Buffalo Bill tirant au galop. — Buffalo Bill im Reiten schiessend.

Hitting composition balls thrown in air with an ordinary Colt's army revolver. (*Shoots.*)

Next on our programme, the Deadwood stage coach, formerly the property of Gilmore, Salsbury & Co., and plying between Deadwood and Cheyenne. This coach has an immortal place in American history, having been baptized many times by fire and blood. The gentleman holding the reins is Mr. John Higby, an old stage driver, and formerly the companion of Hank Monk, of whom you have all probably read. Seated beside him is Mr. John Hancock, known in the West as the Wizard Hunter of the Platte Valley. Broncho Bill will act as out rider, a position he has occupied in earnest many times with credit. Upon the roof of the coach is seated Mr. Con Croner, the Cowboy Sheriff of the Platte, to whose intrepid administration of that office for several consecutive terms covering a period of six years, Lincoln County, Neb., and its vicinity are indebted for the peace and quiet that now reigns. Mr. Croner's efforts have driven out the cattle thief and hoodlum element who formerly infested that section of the country, noticeably, the notorious Middleton gang. The coach will start upon its journey, be attacked from an ambush by a band of fierce and warlike Indians, who in their turn will be repulsed by a party of scouts and cowboys, under the command of Buffalo Bill. Will two or three ladies and gentlemen volunteer to ride as passengers?

After passengers are seated in coach.

It is customary to deliver parting instructions to the driver before he starts on his perilous journey, something in the following fashion: Mr. Higby, I have intrusted you with valuable lives and property. Should you meet with Indians, or other dangers, *en route,* put on the whip, and if possible, save the lives of your passengers. If you are all ready, go!

Coach is driven down track, meets Indians, turns, followed by Indians. Battle back to stand. Cody and cowboys come to rescue. Battle past stand. Exeunt omnes.

Next on our programme, a one-quarter mile race between Sioux boys and on barebacked Indian ponies from the Honorable William F. Cody's ranch at North Platte, Neb., starting at ——

Race as above. Music.

Attack on the ola Deadwood coach by Indians.

Les Indiens attaquant la vieille diligence de Deadwood. — Angriff von Sioux-Indianern auf die alte Postkutsche.

Race between Indian, Cowboy and Vaquero.

Course d'un Cowboy avec un Indien et un Vaquero. — Wettrennen zwischen Indian.,

THE INDIAN DANCE BEFORE MY GUESTS.

I would next call your attention to an exciting race between Mexican thoroughbreds. These animals are bred with great care, and at considerable expense, their original cost being sixteen dollars per doz. All up! No jockeying! Go!

Race as above. Music. "We Won't Come Home till Morning."

A portion of the Pawnee and Wichita tribes will illustrate their native sports and pastimes, giving first the war dance.

War dance by Indians.

Next the grass dance.

Grass dance by Indians.

Next, the scalp dance, in which the women of the tribe are allowed to participate.

Scalp dance by Indians and squaws.

Keep your eyes on the burros!

Burros return. Music. "Home Again!" or "We Never Speak as, Etc."

I have the pleasure of introducing "Mustang Jack," or as the Indians call him "Pet-se-ka-we-cha-cha," the great high jumper. Jack is the champion jumper among the cowboys of the West, and stands ready to jump with anybody in any manner or style for any amount of money. He will give you an exhibition of his skill, jumping over various animals, beginning with the small burro.

Jack jumps over burro.

Jumping twenty-four feet in two jumps, and clearing the burro in the second jump.

Jack jumps as above.

Jumping the Indian pony, Cha-sha-sha-na-po-geo, a feat which gave him his name of "Mustang Jack."

Jumps as above.

Next, jumping the tall white horse, "Doc. Powell," sixteen and a half hands high. The best recorded standing high jump is one of five feet and three inches made by Mr. Johnson of England. In order to clear this horse, Jack is obliged to make a jump of nearly six feet, thus beating the record daily.

Jumps as above.

Indian War Dance.

Danse de guerre des Indiens. — Indianischer Kriegstanz.

Next on our programme the roping, tying, and riding of wild Texan steers by cowboys and Mexicans.

Performance as above.

Next on our programme the riding of a wild elk, by Master Voter Hall, a Feejee Indian from Africa.

Saddled elk ridden as above.

Next on our programme the attack upon a settler's cabin by a band of marauding Indians, and their repulse, by a party of scouts and cowboys, under the command of Buffalo Bill. After our entertainment you are invited to visit the Wild West camp. We thank you for your polite attention, and bid you all good afternoon.

Battle as above. Review before the grand stand. Adieux and dismissal by Mr. Cody.

FINIS